Ultimate Victoria Sponge

There is nothing that represents British Baking as much as a Victoria sponge cake. If you want to be a little more decadent you could add a layer of cream or buttercream as well as the jam.

Prep Time: 25 mins **Cook Time:** 25 mins **Serves:** 8

Ingredients:
* Knob of Unsalted Butter, melted
* 225g Unsalted Butter, softened
* 225g Billington's Golden Caster Sugar
* 4 Large Free-Range Medium Eggs, lightly beaten
* 225g Allinson Nature Friendly Self-Raising Flour, sifted, plus 1 tbsp extra for dusting

For the Filling and Topping:
* 4-6 tbsp good quality Strawberry or Raspberry Jam
* Silver Spoon Caster Sugar, for dusting

Method:
1 Pre-heat the oven to 180°C, fan oven 160°C, Gas 4.

2 Grease 2 x 20cm round tins with the melted butter, and lightly dust with flour. Base line both tins with baking paper.

3 Place the butter in a large mixing bowl and add the sugar. Beat together, preferably with an electric mixer until the mixture is light and fluffy. Do not rush this stage it can take as long as 15 minutes.

4 Add the eggs one at a time, adding a spoonful of the flour if the mixture starts curdling. Fold in the remaining flour with a metal spoon until you have a soft, smooth cake mix.

5 Divide the mixture between the prepared tins, and level the tops with a spatula making a slight dip in the centre to ensure a flat cake once cooked. Bake for about 20-25 minutes or until the cakes are golden brown and spring back when pressed gently.

6 Remove from the oven and cool in the tins for about 5-10 minutes. Remove from the tins and cool completely on a wire rack.

7 Spread the jam onto one cake and carefully sandwich together with the other cake. Dust the top with caster sugar and serve with a fresh pot of tea.

Top Tip:
Think ahead when you make a cake and take the butter out of the fridge for an hour so it is softened before you start making a sponge cake.

Fruit Scones

Warm scones, topped with luscious clotted cream and strawberry jam is as British as Buckingham Palace or cricket on the village green.

Prep Time: 20 mins **Cook Time:** 20 mins **Serves:** 8

Ingredients:

* 250g Allinson Nature Friendly Plain Flour
* 2½ tsp Baking Powder
* 3 tbsp Billington's Golden Caster Sugar
* 40g Unsalted Butter, softened
* 100g Sultanas or Mixed Dried Fruit
* 1 Egg
* 75g Buttermilk

To Serve with:

* Strawberry Jam
* Clotted Cream

Method:

1 Heat the oven to 220°C, fan oven 200°C, Gas 7. Line a baking tray with baking paper.

2 Place the flour, baking powder, sugar and butter into a bowl and rub together with your fingertips until you get a mix resembling breadcrumbs. Mix in the dried fruits.

3 Beat together the egg and buttermilk and stir into the flour mix using a round blade knife. Using slightly floured hands combine to a ball of dough, adding a little more buttermilk if necessary if the dough seems a little dry.

4 Lightly flour a work surface and press the dough to a thickness of 4cm. Use a round 5cm cutter and cut out the scone shapes. Place on the tray leaving a gap between them. Brush the tops with extra buttermilk and sprinkle with caster sugar.

5 Bake for 15-20 minutes until risen and lightly golden brown. Cool slightly on a wire rack.

6 When ready to serve, split and top with jam and clotted cream.

Top Tip:
When cutting out the scones dip the cutter in flour but do not twist the cutter or this may stop the sconces rising evenly. The sign of a perfect scone is that you should be able to split the scones without a knife.
If you are not keen on sultanas substitute with mixed dried fruit, glacé cherries or even make them plain.

Jubilee Cupcakes

These little gems will bring on a great cheer to any street party.

Prep Time: 25 mins plus decoration time   **Cook Time:** 20 mins   **Serves:** 10

Ingredients:

* 125g Unsalted Butter, softened
* 125g Billington's Golden Caster Sugar
* 2 Medium Eggs
* 100g Allinson Nature Friendly Self Raising Flour
* Zest of 1 Unwaxed Lemon
* 2 tbsp of Milk

For the Decorations:

* 50g-75g Silver Spoon Create Ready To Roll Icing in red, white and blue
* Silver Spoon Create Silver Balls
* Silver Spoon Create White Designer Icing
* Silver Spoon Create Lemon Flavour Icing Sugar
* 200g Unsalted Butter, softened

Method:

1 Preheat oven to 200°C, fan oven 180°C, Gas 6. Place 10 large cup cake cases into a muffin tray.

2 Place the butter in a large mixing bowl and add the sugar. Beat together with an electric mixer until the mixture is light and fluffy.

3 Add the eggs one at a time, adding a spoonful of the flour if the mixture starts curdling. Fold in the remaining flour and lemon zest with a metal spoon until you have a soft, smooth cake mix. Add a little milk if the mixture looks stiff.

4 Divide the mixture between the cases. Bake in the oven for about 15-20 minutes or until the cakes is golden brown and springs back when pressed gently.

5 For the topping: Roll the individual coloured ready to roll icing to a thickness of a pound coin and cut out shapes such as crowns or hearts. If you need to stick the silver balls to the decoration use Silver Spoon Create White Designer Icing.

6 Place all the lemon flavoured icing sugar into a large bowl, add two tablespoons of water and mix. Add the butter and beat until thoroughly mixed and smooth. It is easier to make this using an electric mixer to ensure a smooth light butter icing.

7 Spoon the butter icing into a large piping bag fitted with a large star nozzle and pipe a swirl onto the cake. To finish add your chosen icing decoration.

Top Tip:
To pipe swirls on cupcakes, use a large star or plain nozzle, hold the bag vertically and pipe a ring of icing around the edge of the cupcake and work into the middle of the cake slightly overlapping each ring, when you get to the centre of the swirl, push the bag down and draw up sharply to finish..

Union Jack Tray Bake

This would be a centrepiece for any British celebration be it a Diamond Jubilee street party or a gathering to watch the opening of the 2012 Olympics.

Prep Time: 15 mins   **Cook Time:** 30 mins   **Serves:** 15

Ingredients:
* 300g Unsalted Butter, softened, plus a little for greasing
* 300g Billington's Golden Caster Sugar
* 6 Medium Eggs, lightly beaten
* 300g Allinson Nature Friendly Self-Raising Flour
* 1 tsp Nielsen-Massey Vanilla Paste
* 150g Raspberries

For the Topping:
* 200g Unsalted Butter, Softened
* 450g Silver Spoon Icing Sugar
* 1-2 tbsp Milk
* Strawberries
* Blueberries
* Raspberries

Method:
1. Heat oven to 180°C, fan oven 160°C, Gas 4. Grease a 30 x 25cm tin and line with baking paper.
2. Place the butter in a large mixing bowl and add the sugar. Beat together with an electric mixer until the mixture is light and fluffy.
3. Add the eggs one at a time, adding a spoonful of the flour if the mixture starts curdling. Fold in the remaining flour with a metal spoon until you have a soft, smooth cake mix. Stir in vanilla paste. Carefully fold in the raspberries.
4. Spoon the mixture into the tin and bake for 25-35 minutes or until golden and risen. Since this cake is long and wide make sure you check the cake is cooked through by inserting a skewer in the middle of the cake and when it is ready it should come out clean.
5. Cool in the tin, and then transfer onto a cooling rack and cool completely.
6. **For the topping:** Beat the butter and a quarter of icing sugar in a large bowl until soft. Add the remaining icing a little at a time and beat until smooth. Do not add too much icing sugar at a time or your kitchen will be covered with a layer of fine icing sugar.

   Add a little milk and beat the mixture until creamy and smooth. Spread the butter icing over the top and sides of the cake. Find a picture of the Union Jack Flag and recreate the pattern using a selection of sliced strawberries, blueberries and raspberries. Leaving the white butter icing exposed to create a white line. Do not do this too early or the fruits may bleed into the icing.

Top Tip:
If you do not have a cake tin similar to these measurements, just check if any of your roasting trays measure up. Line completely with a double layer of baking paper. If the edges are not perfect you could always trim, as they will be covered with butter icing.

Jam Tarts

What a childhood treat – jam tarts.

Prep Time: 30 mins   **Cook Time:** 20 mins   **Serves:** 12

Ingredients:
* 100g Allinson Nature Friendly Plain Flour
* Pinch of salt
* 55g Unsalted Butter, cubed or an equal mix of butter and lard
* 1-2 tbsp very cold water

For the Filling:
* Raspberry Jam and or lemon curd, for filling

Method:

1 To make pastry place the flour, salt, butter and lard, if using, in a food processor and pulse until the mixture resembles fine breadcrumbs. Through the funnel on the top of the processor, slowly add the water a little at a time until the mixture comes together in a ball. Collect the pastry into a ball and wrap in cling film, chill for 30 minutes.

2 Preheat the oven to 180°C, fan oven 160°C, Gas 4. Lightly grease a 12 hole tart tin with a little butter.

3 Unwrap the pastry onto a lightly floured work surface and roll to a 0.5cm thickness. Using a tart cutter or cup, cut circles from the pastry just slightly bigger than the holes in the prepared tart mould. Gently press one disc into each hole.

4 Place a teaspoon of jam or lemon curd into the pastry lined tins. Be careful not to overfill as the jam will spill out when hot and burn.

5 Bake for 15 minutes or until golden brown. Remove from the oven and leave to cool completely, do not eat while hot or it can burn, the jam stays hot for a long time.

Top Tip:
This recipe is a great introduction to cooking for children. The pastry is so easy to make in the processor. Once they have mastered this they will be ready to help make mince pies for Christmas.

Bakewell Slices

This famous British tart made in the picturesque town of Bakewell in the Derbyshire Peak District. It is a delicious dessert and also makes a delightful afternoon treat.

Prep Time: 45 mins   **Cook Time:** 45 mins   **Serves:** 8-10

For the Pastry:

* 425g Allinson Nature Friendly Plain Flour, plus extra for dusting
* ½ tsp Salt
* 100g Billington's Golden Caster Sugar
* 250g Unsalted Butter
* 50g Ground Almonds
* 1 Free-Range Medium Egg, beaten
* 2 Free-Range Medium Egg Yolks

For the Filling:

* 400g Ground Almonds
* 175g Billington's Golden Caster Sugar
* 8 Free-Range Medium Eggs, beaten
* ½ tsp Nielsen-Massey Almond Extract
* 3 tbsp Raspberry Jam
* 50g Flaked Almonds

Method:

1 For the pastry, place the flour, salt, sugar, butter and almonds into a food processor and pulse until the mixture resembles breadcrumbs.

2 Add the eggs and egg yolks one at a time and pulse until a smooth dough is formed.

3 Wrap the dough in cling film and chill in the fridge for half an hour.

4 Preheat the oven to 180°C, fan oven 160°C, Gas 4.

5 Grease and flour a 30 x 20cm/12 x 8" loose bottom tart tin.

6 Unwrap the chilled pastry and roll out onto a cold, floured work surface. This pastry can be very fragile to handle so work quickly.

7 Line the tart tin with the pastry and trim off any excess. Prick the base with a fork, and then cover the pastry lightly with some baking paper. Cover the paper with baking beans or uncooked rice and place into the oven to bake blind for 15 minutes.

8 Remove from the oven and remove the baking beans. Return to the oven for a further 5 minutes to dry the pastry further.

9 Reduce the oven temperature to 165°C, fan oven 145°C, Gas 2.

10 For the filling, mix together the ground almonds and caster sugar. Add the beaten eggs and almond extract and mix well.

11 When the pastry has cooled spread a generous layer of raspberry jam onto the pastry base.

12 Pour the filling mixture over the raspberry jam to fill the pastry case.

13 Top with flaked almonds, then bake in the oven for 25-30 minutes, or until the filling is baked through and golden-brown all over.

14 Remove from the oven and allow to cool. Cut into slices and serve.

Top Tip:
If time is a little against you can use
ready-made sweet pastry for the base.
If you have an incredible sweet tooth,
cover the top with icing.

Cream Filled Pink Swirled Meringues

These are ideal to make for a party since you can make them a week in advance and store in an airtight container.

Prep Time: 20 mins   **Cook Time:** 2 hrs   **Makes:** 24

Ingredients:
* 3 Egg Whites
* 150g Silver Spoon Caster Sugar
* 1 tsp Nielsen-Massey Rose Water
* 1-2 tsp Silver Spoon Create Colour Creator Pink Food Colouring

For the Topping:
* 150g Raspberries
* 2 tbsp Silver Spoon Icing Sugar
* 150ml Double Cream

Method:
1 Preheat the oven to 120°C, fan oven 100°C, Gas ½.

2 Beat the egg whites in a clean, dry bowl until the whites double in volume and hold peaks. While the whisk is still running add the sugar a tablespoon at a time, until all the sugar is added and the whites are glossy and hold a stiff peak. Use a spatula and scrape all the mixture into the bowl. Fold in the rose water. Do not over beat.

3 Place a dot of the mixture in each corner of the baking paper and line two baking sheets with baking paper using the dots of the meringue to keep the paper in place.

4 Pour about 1 tsp of the pink food colouring onto a saucer and using a wide pastry brush, brush a line of the colouring up the inside of a piping bag. Spoon the meringue mix into the bag.

5 Pipe the meringue into 3.5cm wide swirls or drop the mixture using a teaspoon.

6 Bake in the preheated oven for 1½ hours until they are crisp and lift off the paper easily. Leave to cool in the oven with the door ajar for another hour or even overnight.

7 To make the raspberry coulis, put the raspberries and 1 tbsp icing sugar into the bowl of a food processor and blend to a purée.

8 Set a sieve over a clean bowl and rub the purée through to remove the raspberry pips.

9 To serve, whisk the cream and remaining icing sugar until softly peaked. Swirl in the raspberry coulis. Spoon or pipe the cream onto half the meringues and sandwich with the remaining meringues.

Eccles Cakes

These little currant filled gems are the perfect cake for a picnic – since they are quite robust and travel very well.

Prep Time: 25 mins   **Cook Time:** 15 mins   **Serves:** 20

Ingredients:

* 1 Quantity Rough Puff Pastry as seen in the Sausage Roll recipes (page 53)
* 75g Unsalted Butter, melted
* 125g Billington's Light Muscovado Sugar
* 175g Currants
* ¼ tsp Ground Mixed Spice
* ½ Orange, zest only
* Allinson Nature Friendly Plain Flour, for dusting
* 2 tbsp Milk
* 1 tbsp Silver Spoon Caster Sugar

Method:

1 Preheat the oven to 180°C, fan oven 160°C, Gas 4.

2 For the filling, mix together the melted butter, soft light Muscovado sugar, currants, ground mixed spice and orange zest until well combined.

3 Roll the pastry on a lightly floured work surface. Cut about 20x 8cm discs either using a pastry cutter or a saucer.

4 Place spoonful of the filling in the centre of each of the pastry discs. Brush the edge of each disc with a little cold water, and gather the edges into the centre making a little pouch. Make sure the edges are sealed and you can not see any of the filling. Place the cakes upside down on a baking tray with the join underneath and flatten lightly.

5 Make two small slits in the top of each of the cakes. Brush each of the cakes with a little milk, and then sprinkle over the caster sugar.

6 Bake for 10-12 minutes, or until the pastry is golden-brown.

Top Tip:
You can add mixed peel to the filling. Or if you want to give these Eccles Cakes a contemporary twist why not mix in some sour dried cherries or cranberries.

Spiced Bramley Apple Cake

**This makes the best of a British institution - the Bramley apple.
Serve as part of afternoon tea or with a dollop of crème fraîche.**

Prep Time: 20 mins   **Cook Time:** 1 hr, 15 mins   **Serves:** 8-10

Ingredients:

* 225g Unsalted Butter, softened
* 180g Billington's Light Muscovado Sugar
* 4 Medium Eggs
* 300g Allinson Nature Friendly Plain Flour
* 2 tsp Baking Powder
* ½ tsp Salt
* 2 Bramley Apples, peeled cored and cubed
* 1 tsp Ground Cinnamon
* 1 tsp Ground Nutmeg
* 1 tsp Ground Cardamon, optional
* 200ml Crème Fraîche

For the Topping:

* 1 Bramley Apple, peeled, cored and sliced
* 2 tbsp Lemon Juice
* 2 tbsp Billington's Golden Caster Sugar
* 2 tbsp Smooth Marmalade

Method:

1 Preheat the oven to 180°C, fan oven 160°C, Gas 4. Lightly grease and line the bottom of a 20cm spring form deep tin with baking paper.

2 Place the butter and sugar in a large bowl and beat until light and fluffy. Add the eggs one at a time and continue to beat until light and fluffy.

3 Sift flour, baking powder and salt. Add the flour into the butter mixture in 3 batches alternating with the crème fraîche.

4 Toss the apples with the three spices and fold into the mixture.

5 Pour the batter into the baking tin. Smooth the top.

6 **For the topping:** Place the apple slices in a bowl and add the lemon juice. Toss lightly and drain. Add the caster sugar and toss again being careful not to damage them. Arrange the apple slices on top of the cake and bake for about 1 hour – 1 hour 15 minutes hour or till golden brown and a skewer comes out clean when inserted into the middle of the cake. If the top begins to darken too much cover with a circle of baking paper.

7 Remove from the oven. Let it cool for 10 mins in the pan and then turn it out on the cooling rack.

8 Warm up the orange marmalade in the microwave for 15 seconds and brush it all over the top of the cake.

Top Tip:
You can add a handful of
sultanas to this mixture for an
added fruity element.

Raspberry Ripple Ice Cream

You can not beat homemade ice cream. Once you have mastered the custard you can experiment with lots of other flavours.

Prep Time: 2 hrs   **Chilling and Freezing Time:** preferably overnight

Ingredients:

* 1x 568ml carton Double Cream
* 300ml Milk
* ½ tsp Nielsen-Massey Vanilla Paste
* 6 Large Egg Yolks
* 50g Silver Spoon Caster Sugar
* 4-5 tbsp Askeys Treat Raspberry Sauce
* 1 tbsp Silver Spoon Icing Sugar

To Serve:

* Askeys Wafer Cones
* Askeys Sprinkles

Method:

1. Pour the cream and milk in a heavy based pan. Stir in the vanilla paste. Heat the mixture to just below boiling point.
2. Beat together the egg yolks and sugar preferably with an electric mixer until thick and creamy.
3. Pour the cream mixture on to the egg yolk mixture, whisking constantly. Return the mixture to the pan and heat on a low heat and stir for about 10 minutes or until the custard thickens enough to lightly coat the back of a wooden spoon.
4. Strain the custard into a clean bowl and leave to cool. Place in the fridge until completely cold.
5. Pour the cold custard into an ice cream maker and start churning until the custard starts to thicken and holds it's shape.

   Alternatively, pour the custard into a freezer container, cover and place in the freezer. Remove after 2 hours and whisk well to break up the ice crystals. Return to the freezer. Repeat the process twice more or until the ice cream is extremely thick and holds its shape.
6. Spoon the raspberry sauce through the thick ice cream, making a 'ripple' effect. Cover and freeze overnight or until firm.
7. Remove the ice cream from the freezer 5 minutes before serving. Scoop into balls and serve inside a wafer cone and sprinkle with sprinkles.

Top Tip: Fold in broken biscuits into the thickened custard for an ice cream with a crunch.

Elderflower and Berry Jelly

This not only tastes deliciously fresh it looks as pretty as a picture.

Prep Time: 20 mins plus 2-3 hrs chilling time   **Makes:** 6

Ingredients:

* 400g Mixed Berries, plus a few for decoration
* 4 Gelatine Leaves
* 150ml Elderflower Cordial
* 2 tbsp Silver Spoon Caster Sugar
* 425ml Prosecco or Sparkling Grape Juice, chilled

Method:

1. Spoon a tablespoon of berries into the bottom of 6 glasses and refrigerate.

2. Place the gelatine leaves into a bowl and cover cold water and leave to soak for 10 minutes. Pour the cordial into a bowl. Drain the gelatine and add to the cordial. Sit the bowl over a pan of simmering water and heat until the gelatine is completely dissolved and the mix is syrupy. Add the sugar and stir till dissolved, and then remove the bowl from the heat and let it cool for a few minutes.

3. Pour the Prosecco or sparkling grape juice into your cordial mix, and then pour into the chilled glasses. Chill in the fridge until set.

Top Tip:
Grapes also work really well in this recipe especially if you are making it for a dinner party.

Strawberry Tart

The wonderful flavour of summer that is strawberries is the star attraction of this tart. If you want to make it a little extra special top with white chocolate curls.

Prep Time: 1½ hrs   **Cook Time:** 25 mins   **Serves:** 12

Ingredients:
* 450g Allinson Nature Friendly Plain Flour
* Pinch of Salt
* 2 tbsp Silver Spoon Caster Sugar
* 225g Unsalted Butter, cold and cubed
* 2 Medium Eggs, lightly beaten
* 4-5 tbsp Cold Water
* 1 Egg Yolk, for glazing

For the crème pâtissière:
* 425ml Whole Milk
* 1 tsp Nielsen-Massey Vanilla Extract
* 2 Egg Yolks
* 60g Silver Spoon Caster Sugar
* 40g Allinson Nature Friendly Plain Flour
* 100ml Lightly Whipped Cream

To decorate:
* Strawberries, hulled and halved
* 3-4 tbsp Smooth Strawberry Jam

Method:

1 To make the pastry, place the flour, salt, sugar and butter in a food processor and pulse until the mixture resembles breadcrumbs. Add the beaten egg and water and pulse until the mixture starts coming together. Tip the dough onto a lightly floured surface and work the dough into a ball. Add a little water if the dough feels dry. Wrap the dough in cling film and chill for about 30 minutes. Wrap the dough in cling film and chill for about 30 minutes.

2 Preheat the oven to 200°C, fan oven 180°C, Gas 6. You will also need a 30 x 20cm flan tin.

3 Roll the pastry to fit the flan tin. Carefully use to line the flan tin and chill for 30 minutes. Prick the base with a fork, and line with baking paper. Cover the parchment with baking beans or uncooked rice and bake blind for 15 minutes.

4 Remove the baking paper and return the case to the oven, reducing the temperature to 160°C, fan oven 140°C, Gas 3 for a further 10 minutes. Brush the base of the tart tin with the beaten egg and return to the oven for a further 5 minutes. Remove from the oven and allow to cool.

For the crème pâtissière:

1 Pour the milk into a heavy bottomed pan and bring to a gentle boil over a low heat.

2 In a separate bowl whisk together the vanilla extract, egg yolks and caster sugar until smooth and creamy. Mix in the flour ensuring no lumps of flour have formed. Pour the milk into the egg yolk mixture and whisk well, return to clean pan and heat very gently until the custard thickens.

3 Remove from the heat. Pour the mixture into a clean bowl, cover with cling film and leave to cool.

4 Fold the whipped cream into the cooled custard and spread onto the pastry case and arrange the strawberries over the top.

5 Melt the jam in a small pan and brush or drizzle over the strawberries. Leave to set and serve with plenty of fresh cream.

Top Tip:
Make the pastry shell and crème patisserie beforehand and just assemble when ready to serve.

Sticky Toffee Cupcakes

Sticky Toffee Pudding is always a popular dessert on any restaurant menu, so these cake versions are guaranteed to be a big hit with friends and family.

Prep Time: 20 mins   **Cook Time:** 25 mins   **Makes:** 12

Ingredients:
* 180g Pitted Dried, Chopped Dates
* 150ml Boiling Water
* 80g Unsalted Butter, softened
* 150g Billington's Light Muscovado Sugar
* 2 Medium Eggs, lightly beaten
* 180g Allinsons Nature Friendly Plain Flour
* 1 tsp Bicarbonate of Soda
* ½ tsp Salt
* 1 tsp Nielsen-Massey Vanilla Extract

For the Icing:
* 160g Unsalted Butter, softened
* 200g Billington's Golden Icing Sugar
* 2 tbsp Askeys Treat Toffee Sauce
* 25g Silver Spoon Create Fudge Squares, chopped

Method:

1 Place the dates in a bowl and cover with boiling water. Leave to soak for about 30 minutes or while you carry on making the rest of the cake mixture.

2 Preheat the oven to 180°C, fan oven 160°C, Gas 4.

3 Line a 12 hole muffin tray with baking cases.

4 Beat the butter and sugar in a large bowl until light and fluffy and paler in colour. Add the eggs one at a time, adding a little flour if the mixture looks a little curdled. Fold in the rest of the flour, bicarbonate of soda, salt and vanilla extract with a large metal spoon. Finally fold in the dates mixture.

5 Fill the cake cases to three quarters and bake for 20-25 minutes or until risen and golden brown in colour. They may look darker than normal cup cakes, that is due to the Muscovado sugar that gives them a delicious caramel flavour. Leave to cool on a wire rack while making the icing topping.

For the topping: Beat the butter and quarter of icing sugar in a large bowl until soft. Add the remaining icing a little at a time and beat until smooth. Do not add too much icing sugar at a time or your kitchen will be covered with a fine layer of icing sugar. Swirl in the toffee sauce. Cover the cooled cakes with the icing and sprinkle with the chopped fudge squares.

Top Tip:
If you like the salted caramel flavour add a pinch of salt to the butter icing.

Coffee and Walnut Layer Cake

This is such a classic combination and when making three layers it is an excuse for adding even more of this delicious coffee icing.

Prep Time: 25 mins   **Cook Time:** 25 mins   **Serves:** 6-8

Ingredients:

* 120g Unsalted Butter, softened
* 400g Billington's Golden Caster Sugar
* 360g Allinson Nature Friendly Plain Flour
* 1½ tbsp Baking Powder
* Pinch of Salt
* 350ml milk
* 2 tbsp Coffee Granules mixed with 1 tbsp warm milk
* 3 Medium Eggs
* 2 tbsp Maple Syrup
* 100g Walnuts, chopped

For the Icing:

* 250g Unsalted Butter, softened
* 500g Billington's Golden Icing Sugar
* 2 tbsp Coffee Granules dissolved in 1 tbsp Warm Water

OR

* 2-3 tbsp Nielsen-Massey Coffee Extract

Method:

1 Preheat the oven to 170°C, fan oven 150°C, Gas 3. Grease and base line 3x 20cm sandwich tins.

2 Place the butter, sugar, flour, baking powder and salt in a large bowl and mix together preferably using an electric mixer until you get a crumb consistency.

3 In a jug mix together the milk, coffee, eggs and maple syrup. Slowly add this to the crumb like mixture and gently incorporate and beat until well combined. Fold in the chopped walnuts.

4 Divide the mixture equally between the three tins and bake for 20-25 minutes or until the cakes are golden brown and spring back when pressed gently. Leave to cool slightly in the tin before removing and cooling completely on a cooling rack.

5 While the cake is cooling make the icing: Beat the butter until very soft and slowly start adding the icing sugar, do this a spoonful at a time or you will have an icing sugar cloud in your kitchen. When all the icing sugar has been added, beat until smooth and slightly lighter in colour. Add the coffee and coffee liquor,if using and beat again until fully incorporated. Sandwich the three cake layers with the icing and then cover the top and sides of the cake with remaining icing.
Decorate with halved walnuts.

Classic Shortbread

These are such versatile biscuits – cook a batch just to enjoy at home with a cup of tea, to be decorated at a children's party or even packed up and presented as a gift.

Prep Time: 10 mins plus 30 mins chilling
Cook Time: 12 mins   **Makes:** approx. 10

Ingredients:

* 225g Unsalted Butter, softened
* 75g Silver Spoon Icing Sugar, sifted
* ½ tsp Nielsen-Massey Vanilla Paste
* 225g Allinson Nature Friendly Plain Flour, plus extra for dusting

For the pistachio and chocolate shortbread:

* 75g Shelled Pistachios, very finely chopped
* 50g Silver Spoon Dark Chocolate Flavour Cake Covering, chopped

Method:

1 Place the butter and icing sugar the bowl of a food processor and beat until light and pale. You can do this by hand or using an electric mixer. Beat in the vanilla paste. Sift in the flour and beat until smooth. It will be soft at this point. Remove half the dough and place the dough in cling film and chill for 30 minutes or until firm. Add the pistachios to the remaining biscuit dough and mix until well combined. Now place this dough in cling film and chill for 30 minutes or until firm.

2 Preheat the oven to 180°C, fan oven 160°C, Gas 4. Line two baking sheets with baking paper.

3 Roll out the dough on a lightly floured surface to a thickness of about 5mm, pressing it together if it cracks a bit. Cut out the biscuits using a shaped cutter, re-rolling and cutting out using any trimmings. Lay the cookies on a baking sheet and bake for 10-12 minutes until pale golden. Remove, transfer to a wire rack and leave until cold. Repeat with the other dough.

4 When the pistachio biscuits are cold prepare the chocolate. Place the chocolate in a bowl suspended over a pan of simmering water. Leave the chocolate until just melted. Remove from the heat and beat until the chocolate is fully melted and smooth. Leave to cool slightly and pour into a piping bag. When the biscuits have cooled drizzle with the chocolate. Leave to set completely.

Peanut Butter Cookies

Apparently the traditional criss cross pattern on top of peanut butter cookies is so you can distinguish them from other cookies.

Prep Time: 15 mins   **Cook Time:** 20 mins   **Makes:** 10-12

Ingredients:
* 225g Allinson Nature Friendly Plain Flour
* 1 tsp Baking Powder
* 200g Crunchy Peanut Butter
* 175g Billington's Light Muscovado Sugar
* 110g Unsalted Butter, softened
* 1 Egg

Method:

1 Preheat oven to 180°C, fan oven 160°C, Gas 4. Line two baking sheets with baking paper.

2 Mix together the flour and baking powder.

3 In a large bowl, beat the peanut butter, sugar, and butter until smooth. Add the egg and beat well. Gradually add the flour mix, beating well to combine.

4 Take a tablespoon of dough and roll into balls. Place 4cm apart on the baking sheets. Using a fork, press balls in a crisscross pattern, flattening to a 1cm thickness.

5 Bake until lightly golden for 18-20 minutes. Cool the cookies on a wire rack and enjoy with a cold glass of milk.

Jammy Biscuits

Take a trip down memory lane with these jam and cream sandwich biscuits. They may even be too good for the children.

Prep Time: 20 mins   **Cook Time:** 12 mins   **Makes:** 10 approx.

Ingredients:

* 175g Allinson Nature Friendly Plain Flour
* 125g Cold Unsalted Butter, cut in small pieces
* 50g Billington's Light Muscovado Sugar
* Zest of 1 orange

For the Filling:

* 1 x 125g Silver Spoon Create Strawberry Flavoured Icing Sugar
* 100g butter, softened
* 2-3 tbsp seedless strawberry jam

Method:

1 Place the flour and butter in the bowl of a food processor and pulse until the mixture resembles breadcrumbs.

2 Add the sugar and orange zest, and pulse again until the mixture starts to get sticky. Tip the dough onto a lightly floured surface and lightly knead so the dough comes together to form a smooth ball. Chill for 10 minutes.

3 Preheat the oven to 180°C, fan oven 160°C, Gas 4. Line 2 baking sheets with baking paper.

4 Roll the dough out on a lightly floured surface to a thickness of about 5mm, pressing it together if it cracks a bit. Cut out with 16 x 6cm/5cm cutters, re-rolling until all the dough has been used. Cut out a smaller round shape out of half the rounds.

5 Lay the biscuits on the baking sheets and bake for 10-12 minutes until pale golden. Remove, transfer to a wire rack and leave until cold.

6 Place the strawberry flavoured icing sugar into a large bowl and mix in 1 tbsp warm water. Add the butter and mix together with a blender or whisk until light and fluffy. Spread the icing over the full biscuits and top with a thin layer of jam, top with the remaining biscuits. Leave to set for 30 minutes and then enjoy.

Top Tip:
Flavour the biscuits with vanilla paste, lemon zest or almond essence. If you do not want to make these into a sandwich. You can just cook the whole batch whole.

Sticky Lemon and Poppy seed Cake

Lemon is such a fresh summery flavour and the added poppy seeds give the cakes a rustic touch.

Prep Time: 20 mins   **Cook Time:** 40 mins   **Makes:** 10

Ingredients:
* 175g Unsalted Butter, at room temperature, plus extra for greasing
* 175g Billington's Golden Caster Sugar
* Finely Grated Zest of 2 Large Lemons, reserve one lemon
* 3 Medium Eggs
* 250g Allinson Nature Friendly Self-Raising Flour
* 50g Poppy Seeds
* 4 heaped tbsp Natural Yogurt

For the Filling:
* 75ml water
* 75g Billington's Golden caster sugar, plus extra for spirinkling

Method:
1 Preheat the oven to 180°C, fan oven 160°C, Gas 4. Stand the 10 mini loaf cases on to a baking sheet.

2 Put the butter into a bowl and beat with an electric hand whisk until creamy. Add the sugar and beat until lighter in colour. Add all the zest and then add the eggs one at a time along with a spoonful of flour. Once the last egg has been added add the remaining flour, poppy seeds and yogurt. Fold in carefully.

3 Spoon into the loaf cases and bake for about 30 minutes or until a skewer inserted into the centre of the cake comes out clean.

4 While the cakes are cooking make the lemon syrup: Place the sugar and water into a saucepan and bring to the boil for 2-3 minutes. Add the juice from the reserved lemon. Allow to cool.

5 Once the loaves are baked, brush the sugar syrup over the cakes and sprinkle with extra sugar – allow them to cool completely.

Top Tip:
This mixture will also make one 19cm x 12cm x 9cm deep loaf tin. These would also be delicious drizzled with lemon icing. Mix some icing sugar with lemon juice until you get a thick mixture.

Individual Almond Cherry Cakes

These are a delightful teatime treat – made to be enjoyed with a pot of tea out in the garden.

Prep Time: 20 mins   **Cook Time:** 50 mins   **Serves:** 8-10

Ingredients:

* 200g Unsalted Butter, softened
* 150g Silver Spoon Finest Quality Marzipan
* 150g Billington's Glacé Cherries, natural colour, washed, dried and quartered
* 200g Allinson Nature Friendly Self-Raising Flour
* 200g Billington's Golden Caster Sugar
* 4 Medium Eggs, beaten
* 100g Ground Almonds

For the Decoration:

* 100g Silver Spoon Icing Sugar, sifted
* Warm Water
* 6-12 Billington's Glacé Cherries, natural colour, washed, dried
* Handful Flaked Almonds, lightly toasted

Method:

1 Preheat the oven to 180°C, fan oven 160°C, Gas 4. Lightly butter and line with baking paper 6 individual tins measuring about 7.5cm in diameter and 5.5cm in height.
(If you do not have individual tins you could use washed empty small baked bean cans – just line with greaseproof).

2 Roll the marzipan out on a surface lightly dusted with icing sugar to a thickness of a pound. Cut the marzipan into 6 rounds using the tin as a guide.

3 Place the cherries in a bowl and add a tablespoon of flour. Mix until the cherries are coated. This should hopefully stop the cherries sinking to the bottom.

4 Place the butter, sugar, eggs, ground almonds and remaining flour in a large mixing bowl. Beat with an electric mixer or a wooden spoon until just smooth. Fold in the cherries.

5 Half fill the tins with the cake mixture top with the round of marzipan and then top with the remaining mixture. Level the surface. Bake for 45-50 minutes or until a skewer inserted into the centre comes out clean. Turn out to cool on a wire rack.

6 While the cakes are cooling, make the icing: Place the icing sugar into a large bowl. Add the water and mix until you get a smooth consistently.

7 When the cakes are cooled, drizzle with the icing and top with the cherries and flaked almonds.

Top Tip:
If you are not a fan of marzipan you can easily leave out. This mixture will also make enough for a 1kg loaf tin.

Pecan Brownies

The best brownies should be gooey and chewy in the middle and you can serve as part of a street party or picnic. Also delicious as a dessert served with crème fraîche and a raspberry coulis.

Prep Time: 25 mins   **Cook Time:** 25 mins   **Serves:** 12

Ingredients:

* 250g Unsalted Butter
* 200g Silver Spoon Create Dark Chocolate Flavour Cake Covering
* 50g Pecan Nuts, chopped
* 80g Cocoa Powder, sifted
* 65g Allinson's Nature Friendly Plain Flour, sifted
* 1 tsp Baking Powder
* 360g Billington's Dark Muscovado Sugar
* 100g Silver Spoon Create White Chocolate Chips
* 4 Medium Eggs, beaten

Method:

1. Preheat your oven to 180°C, fan oven 160°C, Gas 4. Line a 25cm square baking tin with baking paper.

2. Place the butter and chocolate in a bowl suspended over a pan of simmering water. Heat gently until just melted. Remove from the heat and beat until smooth. Stir in the pecan nuts.

3. In a separate large bowl, sift together the cocoa powder, flour, baking powder and sugar, add this to the chocolate mixture. Stir together well.

4. Add the chocolate chips and eggs and mix to a soft silky texture.

5. Pour your brownie mix into the baking tray, and bake oven for 35 minutes. The brownie should still have a little movement in the middle, as this is what gives the brownie a chewy gooey texture. Leave to cool and serve in squares.

Top Tip:
You can add a mixture of Silver Spoon Create white, dark and milk chocolate chips to this recipe and replace pecan with any nut of your choice such as macadamia, walnuts or hazelnuts.

Welsh Cakes

These delicious simple cakes were traditionally cooked on a griddle or hot stone but do not worry a heavy based frying pan will do the job just as well.

Prep Time: 20 mins   **Cook Time:** 5-10 mins   **Makes:** 12-14

Ingredients:

* 225g Allinson Nature Friendly Self-Raising Flour, sieved
* 110g Unsalted Butter
* 85g Billington's Golden Caster Sugar, plus extra for sprinkling
* 50g Sultanas or Dried Mixed Fruits
* 1 Egg
* Milk, if needed
* Extra Butter, for greasing

Method:

1 Place the flour into a large bowl, add the butter and rub in until it resembles fine breadcrumbs. Add the sugar, sultanas or dried fruit and then the egg. Mix to combine, then form a ball of dough, using a splash of milk if needed.

2 Roll out the dough until it is 5mm thick and cut into rounds with a 6cm fluted cutter.

3 Rub a heavy based frying pan or a heavy iron griddle with butter and wipe the excess away. Put it on to a direct heat and wait until it heats up, place the Welsh cakes on the griddle and cook for 2 minutes, turn over and cook for a further 2-3 minutes.

4 Remove from the pan and dust with caster sugar while still warm.

Top Tip:
Do not have the temperature too high when cooking Welsh cakes or they will not be cooked through.

Nutty Carrot Cake

This is such an easy cake to make, and is guaranteed to be moist and delicious.

Prep Time: 20 mins   **Cook Time:** 1-1¼ hrs   **Serves:** 10-12

Ingredients:
* 2 Medium Eggs
* 140ml Vegetable Oil
* 200g Billington's Light Muscovado Sugar
* 300g Grated Carrot
* 75g Chopped Hazelnuts, plus a few to decorate
* Finely Grated Zest of 1 Orange
* 180g Allinson Nature Friendly Self Raising Flour
* Pinch of Salt
* ½ tsp Bicarbonate of Soda
* 1 tsp Ground Cinnamon
* ½ tsp Freshly Grated Nutmeg
* 1 Egg
* 2 tsp Mixed Spice

For the orange cream cheese icing:
* 250g Cream Cheese, chilled
* 275g Silver Spoon Icing Sugar, sifted
* Finely Grated Zest of 1 Orange

Method:

1 Preheat the oven to 150°C, fan oven 130°C, Gas 2. Lightly grease and line a 13 x 23cm loaf tin with baking paper.

2 Beat the eggs in a large bowl, add the oil, sugar, grated carrot, chopped nuts and orange zest.

3 Sift in the dry ingredients and beat the mixture together until well mixed.

4 Pour the mixture into the prepared loaf tin and bake in the oven for 1-1¼ hours or until a skewer inserted into the middle comes out clean.

5 Allow to cool in the tin and when cool enough to handle remove from the tin. Cool completely on a wire rack before serving.

For the Icing: beat together the cream cheese and icing sugar and most of the finely grated orange zest and mix to combine. The icing should be smooth and quite thick. Spread the icing evenly over the cooled cake and sprinkle with the remaining orange zest. Leave to set slightly and then cut into slices to serve.

Top Tip:
Replace the chopped nuts with walnuts or pecans. You could always add raisins or sultanas for a fruity addition.

Jubilee Trifle

You could not hold any British event without noble trifle.
Best if you can make the day before so all the flavours blend
together beautifully.

Prep Time: 1 hr 30 mins   **Cook Time:** 25 mins   **Serves:** 8

For the Sponge and Fruit Layer:
* Approx 300g leftover Victoria Sponge
* 2-3 tbsp Strawberry Jam
* 2-3 tbsp Sweet Sherry
* 100g Fresh Blueberries
* 300g Fresh Raspberries
* 300g Fresh Strawberries

For the Custard Layer:
* 280ml Double Cream
* 25g Billington's Golden Caster Sugar
* 3 Egg Yolks
* 1tsp Cornflour

For the Cream Topping:
* 300ml Double Cream
* 2 tbsp Silver Spoon Icing Sugar

To Decorate:
* Blueberries, raspberries and strawberries

Method:

For the Sponge and Fruit Layer:

1 Slice the sponge in half horizontally. Spread the jam over one sponge half and top with the other half. Cut into squares and use the sponge to line the base of a deep glass trifle dish.

2 Spoon over the sherry and leave to soak for a few minutes. Sprinkle over the fruit.

For the Custard Layer:

1 Heat the double cream in a small pan until just boiling. Blend the sugar, egg yolks and cornflour. When the cream is hot but not boiling add to the eggs and mix thoroughly. Pour back into a clean pan and heat gently, stirring continuously until the custard is thickened. Cover with baking paper and leave to cool.

2 When cool, spoon over the fruit layer.

For the Cream Topping:

1 Pour the cream into a large bowl and add the icing sugar. Whisk together using a wire balloon whisk until it holds its shape. Don't over-whisk as the cream may split.

2 Spoon the cream over the trifle and top with blueberries, raspberries and strawberries.

Top Tip:
If you do not have time to make all the elements for this amazing trifle you can use ready-made sponge trifle cake or ready-made custard.

Jaffa Orange Cakes

Tea time would not be the same without the little treats. They are made a little less naughty, through the use of Half Spoon Sugar in this recipe.

Prep Time: 20 mins   **Cook Time:** 20 mins   **Makes:** 8

For the Cakes:
* 2 Free-Range Medium Eggs
* 25g Silver Spoon Half Spoon Sugar
* 50g Allinson Nature Friendly Plain White Flour, sieved
* 1 Sachet Sugar Free Orange Jelly
* 75g Silver Spoon Create Dark Chocolate Chips

Method:
1 Preheat the oven to 180°C, fan oven 160°C, Gas 4. Lightly grease an 8 hole muffin tin.

2 For the cakes, place the eggs and sugar into a large bowl suspended over a pan of simmering water (do not allow the base of the bowl to touch the water). Whisk continuously for 4-5 minutes, or until the mixture is pale, fluffy and leaves a trail when the whisk is removed.

3 Add the flour, beating continuously, until a thick, smooth batter forms.

4 Half-fill each muffin tin with the cake mix. Bake the cakes for 8-10 minutes, or until pale golden-brown and cooked through. Remove from the oven and set the cakes aside, still in their tray, until cool. They may sink a little. Remove the cakes from the tins.

5 Sprinkle the contents of the sugar free jelly into a jug of 285ml boiling water. Stir until dissolved and then make up to 450ml with cold water.

6 Pour the jelly into a shallow-sided tray or dish to form a 1cm layer of jelly. Set aside until completely set.

7 When the jelly has set cut small discs from the layer of jelly, slightly smaller than the diameter of the cakes. Sit one jelly disc on top of each cake.

8 Place the chocolate chips in a bowl suspended over a pan of simmering water and stir until melted. Leave to cool slightly and drizzle over the cakes. Leave until the chocolate is set.

Sausage and Chutney Rolls

There is something quite special about homemade sausage rolls especially if they can be eaten warm. These are ideal for a street party, picnic or just to keep the children fed during the summer holidays.

Prep Time: 2 hours   **Cook Time:** 25 mins   **Makes:** 12

For the Rough Puff Pastry:
* 225g Allinson Nature Friendly Plain Flour
* ½ tsp Salt
* 200g Unsalted Butter, chilled and cubed
* 180ml Ice Cold Water

For the Filling:
* 6 Pork Sausages
* 3 tbsp Apple Chutney
* 1 Egg, beaten
* Coarse Black Pepper

Method:

1 Preheat the oven to 200°C, fan oven 180°C, Gas 6.

2 For the rough puff pastry: Place the flour in a large mixing bowl. Add the salt and butter and mix with a large knife. This is to coat the butter lumps.

3 Gradually pour the water into the flour and butter mixture.

4 Using a round edge knife, cut the mixture and chop the butter into the flour, turning the bowl until the dough comes together. The dough is very wet at this point. Place the dough onto a lightly floured work surface. Roll the dough in one direction to form a rectangle approximately 30 x 20cm. Keep edges straight and even.

5 Fold the top third down to the centre, then the bottom third up. Chill for 10 minutes. Remove from the fridge and with the folded edges to the sides roll the pastry out again in one direction to form a rectangle approximate 30 x 20cm. Keep edges straight and even. Fold as before, cover with cling film and chill for another 10 minutes. Repeat this process a further two times. After the last time chill the pastry for an hour.

6 To make the sausage rolls: With a sharp knife, slit the skins of the sausages and push the meat out into a bowl. Add the chutney and mix well.

7 On a floured work surface, roll the pastry out into a rectangle about 35 x 30cm. Cut lengthways into two long, even rectangles. Roll the sausage mixture into sausage shape with your hands and lay along the centre of each rectangle.

8 Brush the long edge of the pastry with water then fold one side of the pastry over, wrapping the filling inside. Press down with your fingers or a fork to seal the join.

9 Brush with the beaten egg and sprinkle with the black pepper.

10 Cut the long rolls into bite sizes and space them out on a baking tray. Bake in the oven for 25 minutes or until puffed, golden and cooked through. Serve with ketchup and pickles.

Top Tip:
You can use flavoured sausages such as Pork and Apple, Pork and caramelised Onion for delicious simple sausage rolls.

Traditional White Loaf

It is worth making your own bread even if it's just for the amazing aroma it creates in the house.

Prep Time: 2-3 hrs including proving   **Cook Time:** 35-40 mins   **Makes:** 1 loaf

Ingredients:

* 12g (approx. 1 tbsp) Allinson Dried Active Yeast
* 1 tsp Silver Spoon Granulated Sugar
* 500g Allinson Strong White Bread Flour
* 1 tsp Salt
* 1 tbsp Vegetable Oil
* 300ml Hand Hot Water

Method:

1 Place 150ml warm water in a medium size bowl. Sprinkle over the yeast and granulated sugar, whisk well and leave in a warm place until the yeast froths up about 1cm. This will take about 15 minutes.

2 Mix the flour and salt in a large bowl. Stir in the oil. Add the yeast mixture along with a further 150ml of hand hot water. Mix together until a soft dough starts to form.

3 Turn the dough onto a lightly floured surface. Knead for about 10 minutes or until the dough is smooth and elastic. Return the dough to a clean, lightly oiled mixing bowl and cover with cling film or a damp tea towel. Leave in a warm place until doubled in size. Ideally in a warm kitchen, airing cupboard or near a warm oven.

4 Pre-heat the oven to 230°C, fan oven 210°C, Gas 8. Lightly oil a 900g bread tin.

5 Turn the dough on to the work surface again, punch back the dough and knead for 5-10 minutes. Shape the dough into a loaf shape to fit the tin and place in the tin.

6 Cover with a damp tea towel or oiled cling film and allow to rise in a warm place until it has doubled in size and has come to the top of the tin. Sprinkle the dough with a little flour to create a crisp, rustic coating on top of the bread. Place in the centre of the pre-heated oven and bake for 15 minutes then reduce the oven temperature to 200°C, fan oven 180°C, Gas 6 and cook for a further 15-20 minutes until the bread is risen and golden brown and sounds hollow when tapped underneath. Turn out the bread and cool on a wire rack.

For the Sandwiches:

Cream Cheese and Cucumber: Thinly slice ¼ a cucumber. Spread sliced buttered bread with some cream cheese and lightly season with black pepper. Top with the cucumber and then sandwich with another slice of bread. Remove the crusts and cut into triangles.

Cheese and Celery: Finely chop 4 sticks of celery, removing any tough string. Place in a bowl and mix with 150g grated vintage cheddar and 3-4 tbsp mayonnaise. Season with black pepper. Spread over buttered slices of bread and top with another slice of bread. Remove the crusts and cut into fingers.

Ham and Quick Apple Chutney: Heat 1 tablespoon oil and cook 1 small finely chopped onion and 2 diced Granny Smiths for about 10 minutes until softened but still holding their shape. Add ½ tsp mixed spice, 50g Billington's Light Muscovado Sugar and 240ml cider or apple juice. Bring to a boil, scraping any bits from bottom of pan, until the liquid is reduced and slightly thickened. This should take about 5 minutes. Leave to cool slightly. Spread the chutney on buttered slices of bread. Top with thick slices of ham and top with another slice of bread. Remove the crusts and half.

Nutty Stilton and Leek Quiche

Quiche always goes down well and this one combined two of very British flavours.
If blue cheese is not your favourite use Cheddar or any other hard cheese.

Prep Time: 40 mins   **Cook Time:** 50 mins   **Makes:** 1

For the Pastry:
* 250g Allinson Nature Friendly Plain Flour
* 125g Unsalted Butter, chilled and cubed
* 2 tbsp Water, cold

For the Filling:
* 40g Unsalted Butter
* 2 Leeks, washed and chopped
* 1 tbsp Fresh Thyme Leaves
* 3 Medium Eggs, lightly beaten
* 100ml Crème Fraîche
* 100ml Milk
* ¼ tsp Grated Nutmeg
* 3 tbsp Parmesan, finely grated
* 75g Walnuts, lightly toasted and finely chopped
* 125g Stilton, crumbled
* Salt and Freshly Ground Black Pepper

Method:

1 Very lightly grease a round 23cm loose bottom tart tin.

2 Place the flour and butter in the bowl of a food processor and process until it resembles fine breadcrumbs.

3 Start adding the water a tablespoon at a time and process until the dough just starts to come together, adding more water as you go. You may not need to add all the water.

4 Turn the dough onto a lightly floured surface and knead lightly until smooth. Shape into a disc and place in the fridge for 30 minutes to rest.

5 Preheat the oven to 200°C, fan oven 180°C, Gas 6.

6 Roll the pastry on a lightly floured surface to a circle big enough to fit the tart tin. Carefully lower the pastry into the tin pressing it into the edges. Lightly prick the base with a fork. Chill in the fridge for 20 minutes. Line the pastry case with a piece of greaseproof paper and fill with baking beans. Bake the pastry case blind for about 12 minutes. Remove the baking beans. Trim the pastry edges carefully, if necessary.

7 Lightly brush the base of the shell with some of the beaten egg from the filling. Return to the oven for another 5 minutes.

8 Reduce the oven temperature down to 180°C, 350°F, Gas 4.

9 Heat the butter in a large frying pan. Add the leeks and cook until softened but not coloured. Add the chopped thyme, season well with salt and pepper and set aside to cool.

10 Beat together the eggs, crème fraîche and milk. Add the nutmeg and Parmesan and season again with black pepper.

11 Place the leeks in the bottom of the pastry shell and sprinkle with half the walnuts. Top with the Stilton. Pour in the egg mixture, shaking the case lightly so the egg goes into every corner. Sprinkle with the remaining walnuts.

12 Bake the quiche for about 35-40 minutes or until the filling is set and golden brown. Serve hot, warm or cold with a crisp salad.

Top Tip:
When making shortcrust pastry, all your ingredients and equipment should be as cold as possible. It's also important not to over-work the dough when kneading, as it will make the pastry tough.

Mini Pasties

The addition of curry paste gives the filling a contemporary twist and the clotted cream a delicious traditional edge.

Prep Time: 20 mins plus 3 hrs chilling
Cook Time: 50 mins   **Makes:** 6

For the Pastry:
* 350g Allinson Nature Friendly Plain Flour
* 90g Lard
* 90g Unsalted Butter
* 5g Salt
* Approx. 2-3 cold water

For the Filling:
* 450g Good Quality Beef eg. Skirt, chopped
* 1 tbsp Madras Curry Paste
* 450g Potato eg. Maris Piper, peeled and finely diced
* 250g Swede, peeled and finely diced
* 1 Onion, finely chopped
* Seasoning
* 2-3tbsp Clotted Cream

Method:
1 Place the flour into a large bowl and add the lard and butter. Rub together until the mixture resembles fine breadcrumbs.

2 Add the water a little at a time and pulse in a food mixer until the pastry starts coming together and leaves the edges of the bowl. Wrap the pastry and chill in the fridge for 30 minutes this will prevent the pastry shrinking when it is cooked.

3 Preheat the oven to 180°C, fan oven 160°C, Gas 4.

4 Roll the pastry on a lightly floured surface and cut out 6 circles measuring 15cm.

5 Toss the meat in the curry paste. Mix together the vegetables in bowl. Pile the vegetables in the middle of the pastry circles and top with the meat adding plenty of seasoning. Put your dollop of clotted cream on top. Then bring the pastry around and crimp together to form a D shape.

7 Place on a baking sheet and cook for 40-50 minutes or until the pastry has a deep golden colour. Serve warm or cold with a crisp salad.

Top Tip:
The filling you can use here is endless
– beef and Stilton, lamb and carrot
and butternut squash or for vegetarian
just a good selection of vegetables.

Cheesy Pastry Twists

Cheese and pastry is always a great hit. Perfect for a street party, taking on a picnic or make smaller ones to serve with drinks.

Prep Time: 20 mins   **Cook Time:** 20 mins   **Makes Approx:** 12-15

Ingredients:

* Make one quantity of rough puff pastry as seen in the Sausage rolls recipe (page 53)
* 150g Cheddar or Emmental, grated
* 1 Egg, lightly beaten
* Ground Pepper
* A Pinch of Paprika
* 50g Parmesan, finely grated

Method:

1 Pre-heat the oven to 200°C, fan oven 180°C, Gas 6. Lightly grease a baking tray.

2 Roll the pastry on a lightly floured surface to a rectangle about 35 x 25cm with the long side towards you.

3 Brush with beaten egg. Sprinkle liberally with grated Cheddar or Emmental, followed by the ground pepper and paprika.

4 Take your rolling pin and gently roll over the cheese so that it becomes slightly imbedded in the pastry. Fold the pastry in half short end to short end so you get a cheese sandwich. Brush both sides with egg and cut into 1cm strips lengthways. Twist and place on the baking tray. Sprinkle with the Parmesan and black pepper. Bake for 20 minutes or until golden brown.

Top Tip:
You can use any hard cheese for these; you could even add a sprinkling of very finely chopped walnuts.

Cheese and Mustard Scones

These delicious savoury scones are best served warm with a liberal spread of butter.

Prep Time: 20 mins **Cook Time:** 20 mins **Makes:** 12

For the Rough Puff Pastry:

* 225g Allinson Nature Friendly Plain Flour
* 1tbsp Baking Powder
* 50g Unsalted Butter, chilled and diced
* 1 tbsp Thyme Leaves
* ½ tsp English Mustard Powder
* Pinch of Salt and Freshly Ground Black Pepper

* 50g Extra Mature Cheddar, grated
* 25g Parmesan, grated
* 2 Free-Range Medium Eggs
* 3 tbsp Buttermilk, plus a little extra to glaze

Method:

1 Preheat the oven to 180°C, fan oven 160°C, Gas 4.

2 Place the flour and baking powder into a large bowl. Add the butter and using your fingertips rub the butter into the flour until it resembles fine breadcrumbs. You could also do this in a food processor.

3 Add the thyme, mustard powder, seasoning and the grated Cheddar and three quarters of the Parmesan, and mix lightly.

4 Add the eggs and buttermilk and using a round blade knife or pulse in the mixer, mix gently until all the mixture is combined into a dough but do not overwork the mix. Place the dough onto a lightly floured surface and lightly roll or pat the dough to a thickness of 2-3cm. Cut the scones using a 5cm round cutter and place onto a baking sheet. Lightly brush the scones with a little buttermilk and sprinkle with the remaining Parmesan and black pepper.

5 Bake for 20 minutes. Let the scones cool slightly, serve warm with extra wedge of British cheese and chutney.

Top Tip:
Add a few chopped spring onions or chives instead of the thyme. For an added crunch add wholegrain mustard instead of the mustard powder.

We're proud that our sugar comes from British farms

Silver Spoon, the homegrown sugar people, have a great range of sugars that are perfect for all your sweetening needs. Silver Spoon is the only sugar grown in Britain, supporting 1,200 UK farmers and directly contributing to the local economy.

Silver Spoon sugar beet travels an average of only 30 miles from the field to the factory and is then made into our fine range of sugars for British families all over the country.

Silver Spoon have all the sugars you'll need to do some delicious baking, whether it's the icing for your cupcakes or the caster for your Victoria sponge!

From the homegrown sugar people

Allinson

The nation's favourite bread flour...*

but did you know we also make Plain and Self-Raising flours for all your baking needs.

Allinson Founded by Thomas Allinson in 1892

Wholemeal Plain Flour
For pastries, biscuits & crumbles

MADE FROM 100% WHOLEMEAL

Allinson Founded by Thomas Allinson in 1892

Wholemeal Self Raising Flour
For delicious cakes & muffins

Allinson Plain and Self-Raising Flours are expertly milled from British Conservation Grade wheat, making them great for baking.

Allinson Founded by Thomas Allinson in 1892

Nature Friendly

Plain White Flour
For perfect pastries, biscuits and crumbles

Allinson Founded by Thomas Allinson in 1892

Nature Friendly

Self-raising White Flour
For delicious cakes, scones and muffins

BakingMad
everything you want to know about baking

For perfect results time after time use Allinson flour in all of your favourite recipes
www.bakingmad.com

*No 1 in market value share (Nielsen)

BILLINGTON'S

SINCE **1858**

DARK MUSCOVADO
NATURAL UNREFINED CANE SUGAR
IDEAL FOR CHOCOLATE CAKES · BROWNIES · FUD

LIGHT MUSCOVADO
NATURAL UNREFINED CANE SUGAR
IDEAL FOR CAKES · PUDDINGS · COOKIES

MOLASSES
NATURAL UNREFINED CANE SUGAR
IDEAL FOR FRUIT CAKES · MARINADES · CHUTNEYS

DEDICATED TO EXTRAORDINARY TASTE

A good recipe requires the best ingredients and when it comes to sugar this means Billington's unrefined cane sugars. Billington's unrefined sugars are very simply produced with the aim of locking in rather than refining out the natural molasses of the sugar cane. It is this difference which gives unrefined sugar its superior flavour and natural colour.

NIELSEN · MASSEY VANILLAS

Vanilla Specialists

DEDICATED TO PROVIDING THE BEST PURE VANILLA AND PREMIUM GOURMET FLAVOURS FOR OVER 100 YEARS.

silver spoon Create

the icing on the cake

Icing for _every_ decorating occassion

For thousands more recipes visit:

BakingMad.com

everything you want to know about baking

Our BakingMad.com experts are here to help you make the most of your baking.

- For baking inspiration and top tips visit: www.bakingmad.com
- For baking advice, drop us an email at info@bakingmad.com
- Or feel free to contact us on: 0844 880 5944